Making Paper Airplanes

By Amber Lovett

Published in the United States of America by
Cherry Lake Publishing
Ann Arbor, Michigan
www.cherrylakepublishing.com

Series Editor: Kristin Fontichiaro
Photo Credits: Page 20, elPadawan / tinyurl.com/hkz5gm5 /
CC BY-SA 2.0; All other photos by Amber Lovett

Library of Congress Cataloging-in-Publication Data
Names: Lovett, Amber, author.
Title: Making paper airplanes / by Amber Lovett.
Description: Ann Arbor, Michigan : Cherry Lake Publishing, [2017] | Series:
    21st century skills innovation library. Makers as innovators junior |
    Audience: K to grade 3. | Includes bibliographical references and index.
Identifiers: LCCN 2016055219 | ISBN 9781634726962 (lib. bdg.) | ISBN
    9781634727297 (pbk.) | ISBN 9781634727624 (pdf) | ISBN 9781634727952
    (ebook)
Subjects: LCSH: Paper airplanes—Juvenile literature. | Handicraft—Juvenile
    literature.
Classification: LCC TL778 .L68 2017 | DDC 745.592—dc23 LC record available at
    https://lccn.loc.gov/2016055219

Cherry Lake Publishing would like to acknowledge the work of the Partnership for
21st Century Learning. Please visit *www.p21.org* for more information.

Printed in the United States of America
Corporate Graphics

A Note to Adults: Please review the instructions for the activities in this book before allowing children to do them. Be sure to help them with any activities you do not think they can safely complete on their own.

A Note to Kids: Be sure to ask an adult for help with these activities when you need it. Always put your safety first!

Table of Contents

It's easy to make your own paper airplanes. All you need to get started is a sheet of paper!

Why Make a Paper Airplane?

Have you ever wondered how to make a paper airplane? Maybe you want to be a pilot when you grow up. Maybe you have seen your brother or sister making paper airplanes. Maybe you want to see how far your plane will go. Making paper airplanes is easy and fun!

What Is a Maker?

Makers are people who make things. Anyone can be a maker! Some people make things with paper, cardboard, or yarn. Other people make things using computers. Sometimes makers work together at **makerspaces**. As long as you are making something, you can be a maker, too!

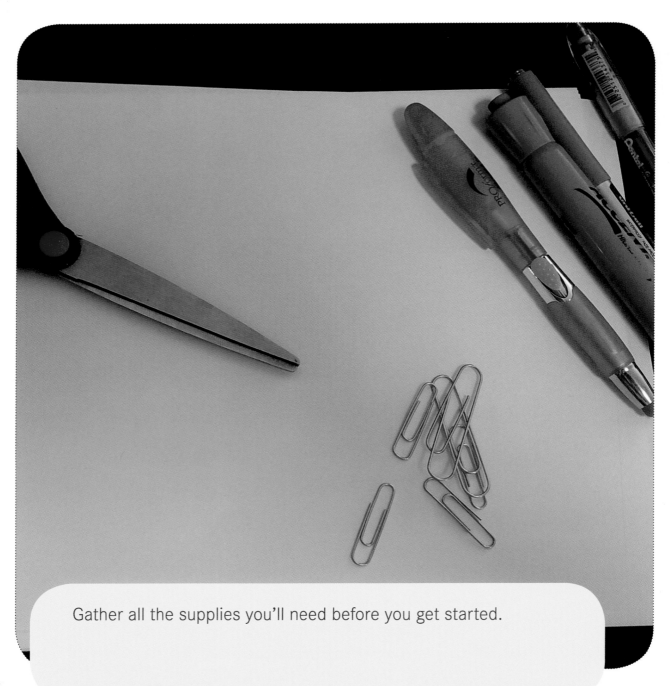

Gather all the supplies you'll need before you get started.

What Do I Need to Make a Paper Airplane?

You probably already have everything you need to make a paper airplane. That's one of the best things about paper airplanes! All you really need is paper and your hands. You might also keep some paper clips nearby. They will help you test how much weight your plane can hold. Pens and markers will help you decorate your plane.

Take your time with each fold. Make sure everything is lined up correctly before you make a crease in the paper.

Starting Out

Grab some paper and find a place to work. Start by folding the paper in half along the long edge. This is called hot-dog style. Always make sure you run your fingertips along the fold to press it down. This will help the paper stay folded.

Types of Paper Airplanes

Did you know there are different kinds of paper airplanes? The kind you are making is called a Bulldog Dart. It will fly far, but it is slow. There are many different types of paper airplanes you can try making. Some fly faster or farther than others.

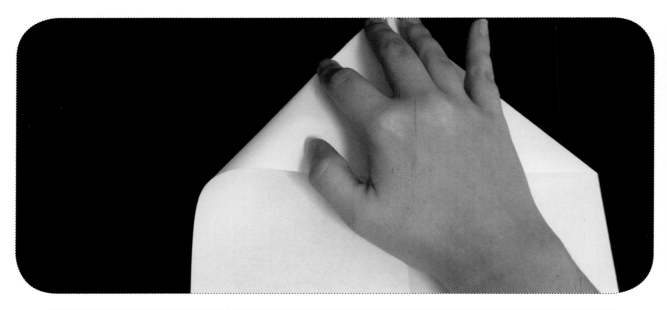

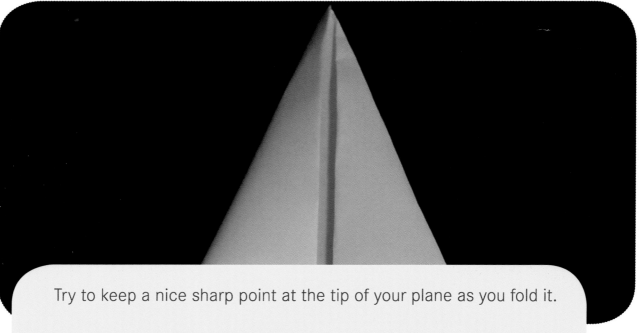

Try to keep a nice sharp point at the tip of your plane as you fold it.

Folding Your Plane

1. Lay your paper down flat.

2. Fold one corner so the top edge lines up with the center crease. Do the same with the other corner.

3. Flip over your paper. The top of your paper will look like a triangle.

4. Fold one of the bottom tips of the triangle so it lines up with the center crease. Do the same with the other side.

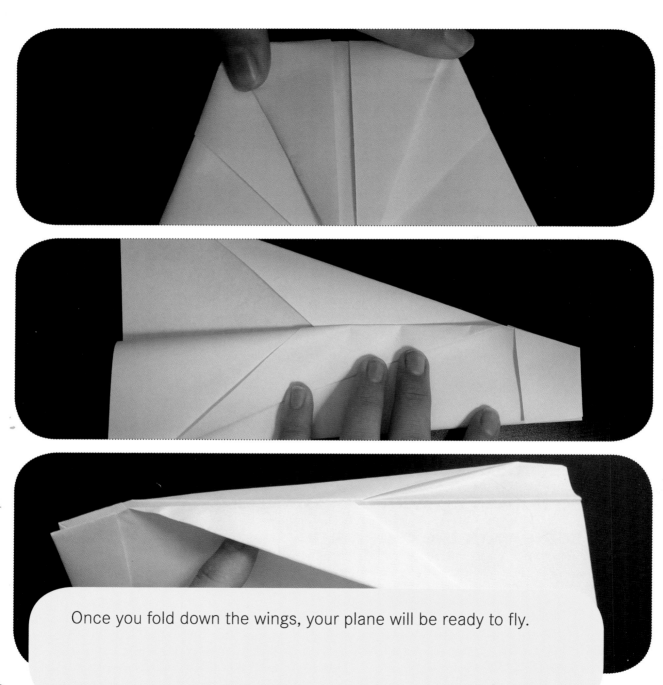

Once you fold down the wings, your plane will be ready to fly.

Finishing Your Plane

5. Fold the pointy tip of your plane down. The tip should line up with the point where the two wings meet.

6. Fold the paper in half.

7. Grab the top corner of one side of your plane. Fold it to line up with the bottom corner. Flip over your plane and do the same thing on the other side.

Gripping your plane in the right spot is key to making it fly far.

Flying Your Plane

When you finish your plane, it is time to test it. Grab your plane by the tip. Don't hold the wings down or your plane will not fly as far. Now throw the plane. Try throwing it from different heights. You can also try throwing it faster or harder. Find out how your plane flies best!

What If My Plane Doesn't Fly?

It's okay if your plane doesn't fly the first time. You can try making a new one. You can also try checking to make sure the plane is folded correctly. Making a good plane takes practice.

Try folding different types of planes to see which ones work best.

Holding Races

Have you built more than one plane? Maybe you have shown your friends how to make a plane. If you have more than one plane, you can hold races. With a friend, try throwing your planes on the count of three. See which plane goes the farthest or the fastest.

Paper clips will change the way your paper airplane flies.

How Can I Make My Plane Better?

There are lots of ways to make your plane better. You can add paper clips to the tip of your plane. Does your plane fly better now? How many paper clips can it hold? You can also give your plane a name. Use art supplies to decorate your plane.

What kinds of paper airplanes will you create next?

What Other Kinds of Planes Can I Make?

Congratulations on making your first paper airplane! Now you can try making other kinds of paper airplanes. Try folding your plane in different ways and see how it flies. You can ask a friend or adult to help you learn a new way. Or go online to find instructions or **templates** for making planes. Find out more in the back of this book!

Glossary

makers (MAY-kurz) creative people who make everything from artwork and useful objects to robots and computer programs

makerspaces (MAY-kur-spay-siz) places where makers gather to share tools, supplies, and advice

templates (TEM-plits) premade patterns you can follow to complete activities

Find Out More

Books

Harbo, Christopher L. *My First Guide to Paper Airplanes*. North Mankato, MN: Capstone Press, 2015.

Roslund, Samantha, and Emily Puckett Rodgers. *Makerspaces*. Ann Arbor, MI: Cherry Lake Publishing, 2014.

Web Sites

Aviation for Kids

www.aviation-for-kids.com

Learn more about the science of how paper airplanes and real planes fly.

Fold'N Fly

www.foldnfly.com

Find instructions for making all kinds of different airplanes.

Fun Paper Airplanes

www.funpaperairplanes.com

Watch videos and download designs to help you make new kinds of planes.

Index

About the Author

Amber Lovett is a teacher and librarian. She received her master's degree in information from the University of Michigan. She likes to make things with her nieces, Leia and Charlotte.